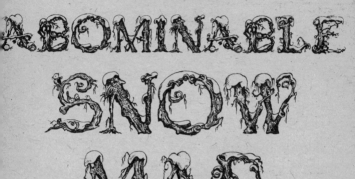

THE ABOMINABLE SNOW MAD

Edited by
Albert B. Feldstein

WARNER BOOKS

A Warner Communications Company

MONKEY BIG BUSINESS DEPT.

There's a wise old expression that goes: "Leave well enough alone!" It seems that everyone in the world has heard the expression except a certain movie studio that gave us a brilliant science-fiction epic a few years back . . . and then proceeded to give us sequel after sequel, each one more tiresome and boring than its predecessor. And it doesn't look like there's any end in sight, because we hear they've got at least two more sequels planned. Well, we think they should put a stop to this monkey business! Yep, it's time they quit

THE MILKING OF THE PLANET THAT WENT APE

ARTIST: MORT DRUCKER   WRITER: ARNIE KOGEN

FIRST CAME THE ORIGINAL...

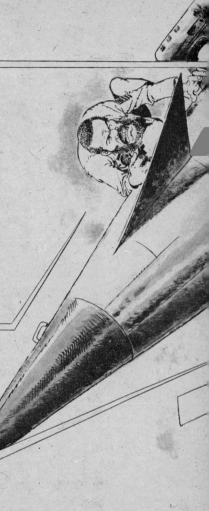

Here we are ... 18 months away from Earth ... and stranded on this strange planet! Just the four of us—three men and a girl!

Wrong! The girl astronaut is ... *yecch* ... dead! Her "Suspended Animation Equipment" failed!

Well, unless one of you guys can dance backwards, our social life is in big trouble!

We'll never get out of this forbidden place! It'll take a MIRACLE!!

Don't look at ME, fellas! I used up my quota of miracles in another movie!

"THE PLANET THAT WENT APE"

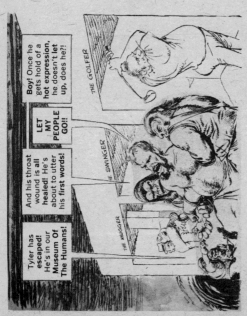

Wow! What a shock ending!

Wrong! This isn't the ending! This is only the BEGINNING! Now we suffer through all the sequels!

What sequels?

Well, the FIRST one is called . . .

Oh, my God! Dr. Zaydius was right! We . . . we shouldn't have come! LOOK . . .

The Statue of Liberty! We're not on another planet! We're on Earth—2000 years LATER!!

And the amazing thing is, there are tourists still walking around in the Statue's head!

Incredible! I wonder how the Statue got destroyed?

Simple! Either it was blasted in a nuclear war . . . or it got MUGGED!! New York City was pretty dangerous in those days!

"UNDERNEATH THE PLANET THAT WENT APE"

Hi! I'm Astronaut Brunt! I was sent here from Earth!

To search for Astronaut Tyler?

That was the official reason! Actually, they couldn't bear to watch me in another of my string of unsuccessful television series!

I am power-mad General Versus! I believe in war! I guess you could call me the very first "Ape Hawk"! I say we attack the humans in the Forbidden Zone!

And I, Dr. Zaydius, forbid you to attack the Forbidden Zone!

And I forbid YOU to forbid ME to attack the Forbidden Zone!

So the dialogue isn't very brilliant! After all, we're only apes! What did they expect . . . Shakespeare?!?

From YOU they did!

"ESCAPING FROM THE PLANET THAT WENT APE"

It's an alien spacecraft! It just landed here . . . off the coast of California!

How convenient! With this next sequel located right at home, and no fantastic sets to worry about, 20th Century Farce will really rake in the ol' profits!

I'm going crazy keeping track of the role-changes! Who plays Carnelius this time?

Good news, folks! I'm back!!

Rowdy McDowelstick! It's YOU!!

Yes! My Agent advised me to take this role again because he doesn't want the public to forget my face!

I'm Sal Moneyo! And MY Agent advised me to take THIS role because he wants the public to REMEMBER mine!!

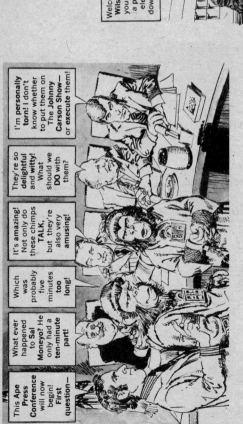

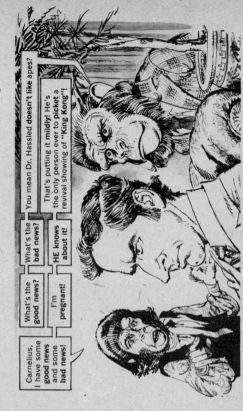

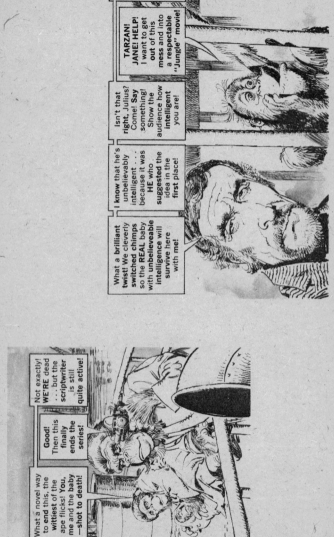

"CONQUERING THE PLANET THAT WENT APE"

Are you sure this is the last one of the series!

No one is sure! But this one is certainly the most ingenius! It will have a vast audience!

Yes! It can be enjoyed by six-year-olds of ALL ages!

Now, remember, Julius! Thees is 1990! We are leeving in a Poleez State! Don't let anyone hear you spick, or we weel be arrested by The Central Security Force!

And don't let anyone hear YOU speak, or we'll be arrested by The Actors Guild!

Thank God he hasn't lost his parents' quick wit and sense of humor!

Of all the apes in the 4 movies so far, you are easily the stupidest! So if I'm going to lead you in a revolt against the humans, you are going to have to follow my advice and not embarrass me! Like from now on, when you put on your shoes and socks, DON'T do it in that order!

We are going to torture you to prove that you are THE talking ape! We have the voltage set on 500! Now, TALK!!

Stubborn, eh, Julius! All right, we'll push the voltage up to 600! Now, TALK!

Okay, it's your last chance! If you DON'T talk, we'll put you into the FIFTH "Planet That Went Ape" sequel!

Four score and seven years ago, our forefathers brought upon this continent a new nation, conceived in . . .

TORTURE COMPUTER
CONTROL

PAT. PENDING
DTY-5626
4353210

BY
MATTEL

LOW MED HIGH

Look! The apes are revolting!

Well, let's say they're a bit tacky!

No, they're rioting, looting and burning! Gee, when I trained for Gorilla Warfare, I never dreamed I'd really get to use it!

They don't stand a chance! We've got sophisticated weapons, electronic computers, and an army of 8000 men!

But Julius is brilliant! He has an arsenal of weapons that just might destroy us!

WHAT weapons!

He's got 8000 banana peels!

Well, Julius, your banana peel trick worked! You've won! Now that you've taken over, what are your plans?

It beats me! I'm not THAT intelligent! I won't know myself until the sequel!

ONE DAY

AT A SEANCE

Who Knows What Evils Lurk In The Hearts Of Men?

THE SHADOW KNOWS

WRITER & ARTIST: SERGIO ARAGONES

ONE EVENING AT A MASQUERADE PARTY

THE LIGHTER SIDE OF...

WEEK-ENDS

ARTIST & WRITER: DAVE BERG

Are **you** still **out** here?!

Huh? Oh—yeah! **You** know how I am! I can't sleep a **wink** until the kids come home from their dates safe and sound!

Just look at the **time!** You'd think they'd be **considerate**, knowing what a **worrier** I am, and come home **early** for once!

But, **no!** Every week-end, it's **the same thing!** And I have to sit here like a wide-eyed **sentinel** ... staring at the **front door!**

I got **news** for you, my wide-eyed sentinel! The kids have been **home** and asleep for **two hours!**

Boy, have I got a **busy week-end** planned! I'm gonna **fix** all the **things** around this house that need **fixing!!**

I'm gonna fix that **leaky faucet** in the sink, repair the **broken back stairs**, cement the **crack** in the basement, rake up the **leaves**, and paint the **playroom!**

Hey! What are you doing, lying around!? What happened to all those **things** you were going to do?

Oh, I'm leaving them all till **next** Saturday—

—when I **don't** have such a **busy week-end** planned!

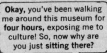

Hoo-boy! Am I exhausted! I have **charlie horse** of my **entire body!** Got up at **5 A.M.** Saturday, drove **180 miles** to the **Ski Lodge,** and spent the whole day on the **slopes,** dodging trees and wiping out!

Spent half the **night boozing it up, making out** and **dancing like a nut!** Got up early **this** morning and spent **another** day **dodging trees** and **wiping out!**

Then, that long drive **home,** and now every bone in my body **aches!**

If a weekend like that knocks you out so **much,** why did you go?

I needed the rest!!

Can you **actually conceive** of the **advancements** that have been made in **travel**? Here we are, about to travel **three thousand miles** to **Europe** and **back**, all in **one week-end**!

It **IS** amazing! And **speaking** of traveling, I **must** borrow a **traveling bag** from Harriet Moran! This **old** one of ours is **shot!** Would you run over and **get** it for me?

Where does she **live**?

Just around the corner!

Forget it! It's **too far!!**

It says here that many people **hate** week-ends and **can't wait** for **Monday morning** because they don't know what to **do** with all that **free time!**

Who ever **wrote** that article was writing about **YOU!** You haven't the **imagination** or the **get-up-and-go** necessary to know what to do with **your** two days off!

I DO SO know what to do with my week-ends!

David Berg

I sit around **hating** them!!

This ode to his favorite Monday night commentator is a good example of the type of idiocy MAD sports freak, Frank Jacobs, is

HOWARD

(with apologies to Ernest Lawrence Thayer)

It looked extremely dismal
    for the TV fans that night;
The game was dull in color,
    even worse in black-and-white;
So, when Dallas missed three field goals
    and the Vikings couldn't score,
The viewers rightly muttered
    that the contest was a bore.

offering in his all-new paperback, "MAD About Sports." So con-
sider yourself warned about this "Humor In A Jock-ular Vein."

AT THE MIKE

ARTIST: JACK DAVIS

WRITER: FRANK JACOBS

But Howard had a cold that night
  and couldn't make the game;
'Twas clear without his acid tongue
  the show was not the same;
Throughout the land from coast to coast
  the viewers fumed and frowned;
A few, in fact, expressed the thought
  of turning off the sound.

Up in the booth was Gifford,
   botching up the play-by-play,
While Dandy Don beside him
   barely had a thing to say;
They tried their hand at making jokes,
   but anyone could tell
They sorely missed the Gabby One,
   the talker named Cosell.

The network switchboard buzzed with calls
  —nine-tenths of them irate—
"We want Cosell," fans screamed, "for he's
  the man we love to hate!"
The network brass behind the scenes
  looked outwardly quite calm,
Though inwardly each bigwig knew
  the evening was a bomb.

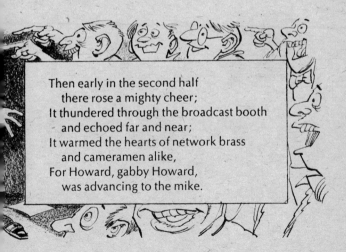

Then early in the second half
   there rose a mighty cheer;
It thundered through the broadcast booth
   and echoed far and near;
It warmed the hearts of network brass
   and cameramen alike,
For Howard, gabby Howard,
   was advancing to the mike.

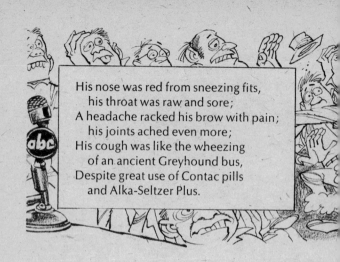

His nose was red from sneezing fits,
  his throat was raw and sore;
A headache racked his brow with pain;
  his joints ached even more;
His cough was like the wheezing
  of an ancient Greyhound bus,
Despite great use of Contac pills
  and Alka-Seltzer Plus.

He flashed a silken handkerchief
 and gave his nose a blow,
Then made his way across the booth
 to watch the play below;
He coolly scanned the first-half stats
 to see which men had played,
Then jotted down the key mistakes
 each quarterback had made.

"He's back!" exclaimed the TV fans,
    as Gifford broke the news,
"The game won't be a bore at all
    with *him* to give his views!"
And then the nation settled back
    to hear the pithy quips,
Those rich and rolling phrases which
    would fall from Howard's lips.

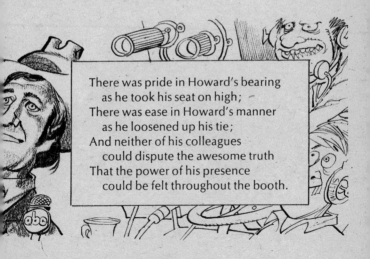

There was pride in Howard's bearing
   as he took his seat on high;
There was ease in Howard's manner
   as he loosened up his tie;
And neither of his colleagues
   could dispute the awesome truth
That the power of his presence
   could be felt throughout the booth.

A glint has come to Howard's eyes,
    his tongue is poised to strike;
His hand is raised to make a point,
    he leans into his mike;
And now we feel the fury
    of that mighty mind of his—
And now the air is shattered
    as he tells it like it is.

Oh, somewhere in this favored land
    there is a happy place
Where folks are watching re-runs
    of "I Spy" and "Lost In Space";
And somewhere there are TV sets
    around which folks rejoice;
But there is no joy in football
    —gabby Howard's lost his voice.

A few issues back (MAD #146, to be exact, nosey!), we interviewed the typical Middle-American *conservative* family. Seeing how many people we infuriated, we couldn't resist the temptation to step on some toes of the *left* foot...as....

MAD INTERVIEWS A TYPICAL

LIBERAL FAMILY

ARTIST: PAUL COKER, JR.   WRITER: LOU SILVERSTONE

Good afternoon, Mr. and Mrs. Heartbleed! I'm **William F. Bugeyes** from **MAD Magazine**, and I'd like to get your views on some of the **problems** facing our nation today!
Welcome to **New Leftchester,** Bill! And please . . . you'll **have** to pardon this **mess** but we're getting ready for a march on **Washington!**
We're **demanding school busing** because we feel it's the **only** way to create **racial balance** in our **Public Schools!**
Are **your** children being bused to school?
No, our kids go to **Private School!** They're picked up by a **service!** But if they **did** attend public school, we would **insist** that they be **bused!** Oh, **absolutely!**
BUSING IS THE WAY
2-4-6-8 BUSING HELPS
BUS OUR

There DOES seem to be quite a number of Black parents here!
Uh—these aren't exactly parents, Bill! Actually, they're chauffeurs, housekeepers, nurses and maids—waiting to pick up their employers' children!
I see! Tell me, do ANY Blacks attend this school?
Bill, there is at least one minority child placed in each class! And not just your common, everyday minorities like Blacks and Puerto Ricans! We've got Indians, Chinese, Italians—even an Eskimo boy! You have no idea how much it costs to fly him from Alaska!
All these underprivileged children are here on Full Scholarships, paid for by us—the "Parents Group"! It makes one feel good to help children of those less fortunate than one's self!
AND, of course, all the money we contribute is tax-deductible!

Listen, you bring me home **Sidney Poitier** and I'll give you my blessings!

Then why are YOU acting the way **Spencer Tracy** did!

And remember when we saw "Guess **Who's Coming To Dinner**"? Didn't I say that Spencer Tracy was wrong in opposing his daughter's marriage to Sidney Poitier? Does that sound like a bigot?

You know I never interfere, Nadja! But you're too **young** to go steady!

I'm **26 years old!** This has nothing to do with age! The truth is you're prejudiced!

Now you've gone too far! **Me . . . ?!** Prejudiced . . . ?! Why, I even put NAACP seals on all of my Christmas cards!

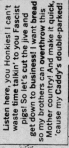

ONE DAY IN THE NORTH WOODS

DISTINCTIVE
ANNC

FROM A LIBERATED WOMAN

Ms. Samantha Rustgrease
Unequivocally Announces
The Satisfactory Signing
Of a Marriage Contract
With
Harvey (nee Schnook) Rustgrease
The Details of Which
Include
Separate Bank Accounts,
Separate Apartments
And a Bill of Rights to Cover
The Couple's Contrasting
Life Styles
And Visiting Rights with Each Other
Tuesdays and Alternate Fridays

WEDDING
UNCEMENTS

WRITER: FRANK JACOBS

FROM A LIBERATED MAN

Monte McHugh
Is Tickled Pink to Announce
After Four Years of Paying
Nine Hundred and Fifty Dollars per Month
In Alimony
He Can Swing Again
Following the Marriage of His Ex-Wife
Belinda
To T. Bascomb Schlepp

FROM PROUD PARENTS

Mr. and Mrs. Cyrus Mumbleman
Not To Be Outdone
By The Fliegheim Wedding Last Year
Proudly Announce The Social Event
Of The Decade
The Marriage Of
Their Delight, Their Darling
Rosalie
To Future Supreme Court Judge Ronald Scurmley
The Cost of the Entire Affair
To Exceed Fourteen Thousand Dollars
Not Counting the Price
Of Arthur Fiedler and the Boston Pops
The Cast of "Holiday On Ice"
The Flying Wallendas
And George Jessel
On Sunday, the Tenth of June
Nineteen Hundred and Seventy-Three
Madison Square Garden

FROM HAPPY PARENTS

Mr. Monroe Spritzer
President of Spritzer Industries
And His Wife, Jeanine,
Realizing the Slim Chance
Of Ever Unloading
Their Fat, Stupid Mouth of a Daughter
Estelle
Are Pleased to Announce
The Acceptance of
Marvin Glieb
As Husband and Executive Vice-President
Through an Agreement Signed
On Tuesday, the Sixth of February
Nineteen Hundred and Seventy-Three

FROM LOYAL PARENTS

Mr. and Mrs. Geoffrey Farfel
Feel Compelled to Announce
The Rather Hastily Arranged Marriage
Of Their Daughter
Melba
To Fortune-Hunter Pierre LaDrecque
In The Maternity Ward Chapel
Mercy Hospital
On Wednesday, the Eighteenth of April
Nineteen Hundred and Seventy-Three

FROM A FUTURE BRIDE

Miss Veronica Hotstrut
Is Pleased to Announce
That Despite her Impending Marriage
To Eighty-Two-Year-Old
Zinc Tycoon
G. Godfrey Grint
She is Still Very Much in Action

FROM DISTRESSED PARENTS

Mr. and Mrs. Oswald Dinwiddie
Have No Choice but to Announce
The Nude Wedding
And Subsequent Orgy
Of Their Daughter
Quandra
To Milton ("The Head") Eggblatt
At High Noon
On Monday, the Twenty-Eighth of May
Nineteen Hundred and Seventy-Three
Times Square

FROM VERY DISTRESSED PARENTS

Mr. and Mrs. S. Thaddeus Wicks
Announce the Disowning
Of Their Daughter
Clarice
Following Her Marriage to
Igor ("God") Mishkin
And Apostles
Cosmo Calhoun and
Lester ("Speed") Quigley
Sometime Last Year
At the
Children of the Enchanted Flower Commune
Taos, New Mexico

FROM TOTALLY DISTRESSED PARENTS

Major General and Mrs. Styles Wilberforce
Are Forced by the Rules of Etiquette
To Announce the Marriage
Of Their Only Son
Charles
To Herman Raffensberger

FROM A DELIGHTED COUPLE

Gloria and Harold Himbersham
Are Overjoyed to Announce
That Gloria's Widowed Mother
Gertrude Grintz
After Living With Them
For Eight Horrible Years
Has, Following a West Indies Cruise,
Landed a Second Husband
Retired Furrier Morris Blemish
And Will Move Immediately,
Thank God,
From Their House in Connecticut
To a Condominium
In Fort Lauderdale

FROM A FILM STAR.

Renowned Motion Picture Star
And International Beauty
Rhonda Vapp
Is Delighted To Announce
Her _Sixth_ Marriage
To _Oilman Clint Sturdley_
On _Sunday_ The _Tenth_ Of _December_
Nineteen Hundred And _Seventy-Three_

FROM A MAFIA CHIEF

Don Vittorio Collazo
Founder, Godfather
And Supreme Being
Of The Collazo Family
Regrets to Announce
The Permanent Postponement
Of The Wedding of his Daughter
Maria
Owing to the Sudden Disappearance
Of Bridegroom Carlo Lambretti
East River
On Tuesday, the Eighth of January
Nineteen Hundred and Seventy-Three

FROM AN ESPIONAGE AGENT

K341 AND "SUNFLOWER"
CAUTIOUSLY DISCLOSE
THE CARRYING OUT OF
"OPERATION ALTAR"
INVOLVING THE APPARENT MARRIAGE
OF THEIR DAUGHTER
"TOPAZ"
TO DOUBLE AGENT H97
AT THE APPOINTED HOUR
AT THE USUAL PLACE
UNLESS FOLLOWED

FROM A GOSSIP COLUMNIST

Waldo ["*Broadway Beat*"] *Wickles*
And B.W. *(Beautiful Wife)*
Reveal it's Wedding Bells
For Daughter Esther
Who'll Middle-Aisle It
With Lance Freebish
(He's the Blintz Biggie)
Around Noonish This Saddy
St. Pat's
(Remember—you heard it here first!)

FROM A BRITISH NOBLEMAN

His Grace
The Duke of Flutney
Fifty-Seventh in Line to the British Throne
Is Relieved to Announce
The End of His Impoverishment
And the Rescue of his Ancestral Home
Rancid Oaks
From Creditors
Following his Marriage of Convenience
To American Lard Heiress
Mary Jane Muncrief
On Sunday, the Fifteenth of April
Nineteen Hundred and Seventy-Three

Cheyenne Geldings Owner Cyrus Wiltfang
And Wife Harriet
Request Your Presence
At The Outright Release
Of Their Daughter
Camilla
To Linebacker Ronnie Bushwater
Obtained from the Memphis Rabbits
For Thirty Thousand Dollars
A Running Back
And a Future Fifth-Round Draft Choice
On Sunday, the Seventh of October
At Halftime
Of the Cheyenne-Memphis Game
Gelding Stadium

Big Savings

ONE DAY ONLY!
SATURDAY AT 2 P.M!
Mr. and Mrs. **HONEST JOHN** Mulvaney
Offer **A ONCE-IN-A-LIFETIME**
FAMILY
CLEARANCE
Namely Their Daughters,
BEATRICE,
LILLIAN
and
MARY BETH
Offered *AS IS*
To The First Takers!
ALL TRANSACTIONS C.O.D!
PHONE ORDERS NOT ACCEPTED!
Free Parking With Any Wedding Gift
Costing Over $25!
Main St. Outlet

Hey gang! Here we go with another MAD "Hate Book," . . . those literary gems calculated to make you feel better by helping you blow off steam about your pet hates. Since it's that time of year again, why not fortify yourself by blowing off steam with

THE
MAD
CHRISTMAS
HATE
BOOK

ARTIST & WRITER: AL JAFFEE

DON'T YOU HATE...

... Christmas music that starts right after Thanksgiving, and practically drives you out of your mind by Dec. 25th.

DON'T YOU HATE...

... all those phony, greedy grins from the service people who are absolutely miserable to you the rest of the year.

DON'T YOU HATE...

... having the smallest feet in the family.

DON'T YOU HATE...

... having to explain all the Santa Clauses to your 5-year-old.

DON'T YOU HATE...

. . . finding that your most wanted gift is damaged,
and must be re-packed and returned to the store.

DON'T YOU HATE...

. . . getting a whole batch of Christmas cards, at the
very last minute, from people you didn't send any to.

DON'T YOU HATE...

. . . waiting for a standby seat as the time for getting home by Christmas is fast running out.

DON'T YOU HATE...

. . . when your class is preparing religious Christmas displays and rehearsing the Christmas Pageant . . . and you're Jewish.

DON'T YOU HATE . . .

. . . gifts that need to be assembled.

DON'T YOU HATE . . .

. . . getting gifts that needed to be assembled.

DON'T YOU HATE...

. . . getting a turkey (or a bottle) instead
of that big cash bonus you were hoping for.

DON'T YOU HATE...

. . . exchanging gifts with your new heartthrob, and finding
out she spent ten times more on yours than you did on hers.

DON'T YOU HATE...

... getting a ton of homework to do over the Christmas holidays.

DON'T YOU HATE...

... spending Christmas in a warm climate.

DON'T YOU HATE...

... getting a gift you have to wait six months to use.

DON'T YOU HATE...

... getting gifts you're forbidden to use in the house.

DON'T YOU HATE...

... having to work on Christmas day.

DON'T YOU HATE...

... bumping into the person whose gift you are in the process of returning.

DON'T YOU HATE...

... rushing out to show off your new 3-speed bike, and the kid across the street just got a new 10-speed bike.

DON'T YOU HATE...

JANUARY SALE EVERY ITEM IN THIS STORE 50% OFF

... those After-Christmas Sales that cut prices in half for gifts you'll still be paying for next June.

ONE NIGHT
IN A BAR

ALONG
THE
HIGHWAY

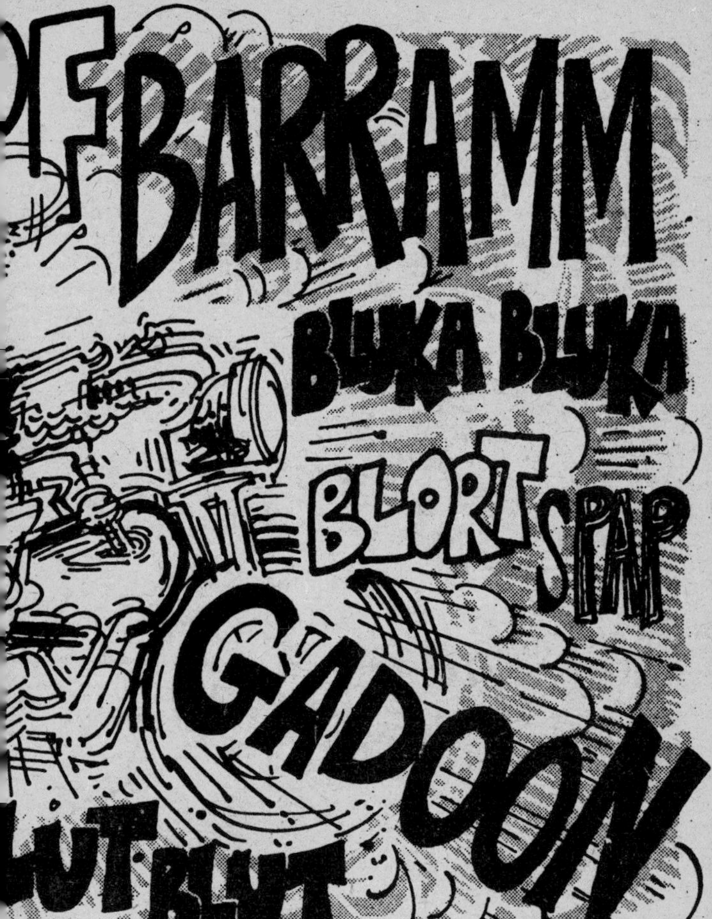
BARRAMM
BLUKA BLUKA
BLORT
SPAP
GADOON
BLUT

A MAD LOOK AT TARZAN

ARTIST: JACK DAVIS

WRITER: DON EDWING

HELP!

Man . . . you're lucky you didn't cut your **head** off!

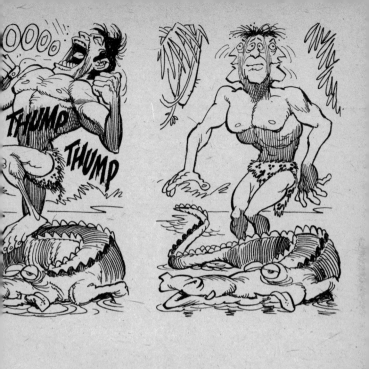

OOOK!
OOOK!

In an effort to get more young men to volunteer, the Armed Services are resorting to new and varied incentive plans. For example, you can sign up to serve with your friends (if you have any). Or you can get a written guarantee that your Army job will be in the career field of your choice (like Cleaning Latrines). And you can wear your hair any way that you want (although spit-curls are still frowned upon). The Navy recently announced that from now on, all their ships are going to be made "homier." They're even talking about assigning female personnel to sea duty . . . which should make them ships about as "homey" as they can get! Anyway, since this "come-on trend" seems to work, we may soon be seeing these

FUTURE
ENLISTMENT
POSTERS

ARTIST: BOB CLARKE
WRITERS: DICK De BARTOLO & DONALD K. EPSTEIN

If You Hate War, Violence, Noise and Bloodshed...
JOIN THE ARMY'S NEW
Dove Division

MAKE PAPER FLOWER CENTERPIECE FOR MESS HALL TABLES

PAINT PEACE SIGNS ON ARMY EQUIPMENT

SEND LOVE BEADS TO THE ENEMY

WRITE LETTERS TO YOUR BATTLE-WEARY FELLOW G.I.'S IN THE BATTLE ZONES ON COLLEGE CAMPUSES

EUROPE ON $10 A DAY*

AND YOU DON'T PAY US...WE PAY YOU!

JOIN THE U.S. ARMY
TRAVEL CLUB

★ WE PAY ALL TRANSPORTATION COSTS
★ WE SUPPLY A NEW TRAVEL WARDROBE
★ NO TIPPING OR GRATUITIES—EVER

*Based on multiple occupancy, 40 in a
barracks, with 3 mess hall meals a day.

NOTE: WE RESERVE THE RIGHT TO SUBSTITUTE SOME EXOTIC ASIAN COUNTRY
LIKE VIETNAM IF ACCOMMODATIONS IN EUROPEAN COUNTRIES ARE FILLED UP.

IF YOU'VE GOT 40 HOURS A WEEK TO SPARE, YOU CAN FULFILL YOUR PATRIOTIC DUTY IN THE NEW...

Monday-To-Friday
(9-to-5)
ARMY

| ALL UNION HOLIDAYS | FREE ATTACHE CASE | KEY TO THE EXECUTIVE LATRINE | USE OF YOUR OWN 9-TON* BUSINESS CAR |

Yes, in Uncle Sam's new "Monday-to-Friday, 9-to-5 Army" you don't have to work any harder or longer than your buddies in the Business World! And if, one night, you have to stay late to finish up some war, you'll get time-and-a-half for overtime!

*YOUR CHOICE OF M-60 TANK OR M-113 APC CARRIER

THE LIGHTER SIDE OF... FUN

ARTIST & WRITER: DAVE BERG

IN THE SUN

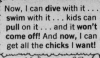

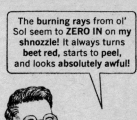

Will you **look** at **that?!?** All Winter long, with the **heavy coats** and **jackets**, you can't tell the **difference** between **girls** and **boys** from the back!

And now that it's **Summer**, even with the **abbreviated clothes**, you **STILL** can't tell the difference!

David Berg

You mean you **really** can't tell the difference between that **boy** and that **girl** from the **back**! Man, are you **dumb**! It's so . . . so **obvious!!**

The **BOY** is the one with the **HIGH HEELS!!**

Ever meet a "Bigot"? Ever try to talk sense to him?
If you have, then you know it's a losing proposition.
Because no matter what you say, he has an answer

YOU NEVER

WITH

ARTIST: PAUL COKER, JR.

that supports his warped point of view. If you don't believe it, then try reading the following examples which clearly demonstrate exactly why . . .

CAN WIN

A BIGOT!

He hit a home run!

Whaddya expect! All them Coons are **strong as apes!** Comes from all those years in the **jungles!**

WRITER: FRANK JACOBS

KNIFIN'
FALK
DEPT.

There have been many famous fictional Detectives through the years, and each has had his own special technique for solving a crime.

F'rinstance, there was Sherlock Holmes who relied on cold logic and British common sense . . .

I say, Holmes! How did you know that Sir Thomas's butler, Baskerville, was the murderer?

Elementary, my dear Watson! Sir Thomas was poisoned by an ordinary tea bag! Baskerville was the only one who knew that Sir Thomas had been bitten by the deadly Teatea fly while he was stationed in India, and that if he ever drank tea, it would be fatal!

Impossible, Holmes! I've had tea with Sir Thomas on numerous occasions!

YOU'VE had tea, Watson! But the tea bags Sir Thomas used were actually filled with dehydrated Scotch! Baskerville substituted a real tea bag!

Brilliant, Holmes! Absolutely brilliant!

And there was Mike Hammer with his American approach . . .

BLAM
BLAM

There was Charlie Chan with his inscrutable reasoning . . .

Gee, Pop! This is a tough case! There are no fingerprints on the murder weapon!

That is correct, Number One Son, Which reminds me of old Chinese proverb: "Man who wear gloves no leave finger smears!" Honorable Rocky here is only one wearing gloves . . . therefore HE is murderer!

Let's go, Rocky . . .

But enough of the crime-fighters of the past! Today, we have a new style TV Detective with his own unique method of solving cases. You'll see what we mean as we take a MAD look at…

CLODUMBO

ARTIST: ANGELO TORRES

WRITE: LOU SILVERSTONE

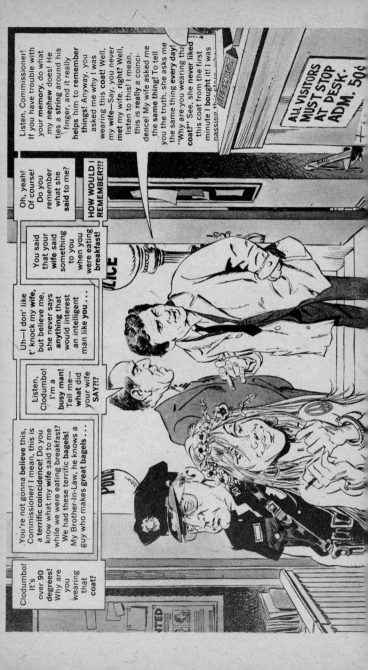

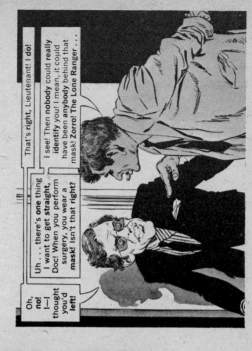

No kidding! Is he . . .? I'm really sorry to hear that! Well, I guess you can't win 'em all, eh, Doc? Uh—you wouldn't happen to have an ash tray around here, would you? Never mind! I'll use this—

Hey, what's the matter, Doc? You got a headache? Listen, I know you're a Doctor, and I don't want to tell you your business, but I think you been working too hard! You gotta relax! Why don't you take this pretty Nurse out to a Drive-In, or for a Pizza! I'll clean up here! You run along!
Lieutenant, I already have a girl, and we're going to the theater tonight! That's one place you can't follow me! The play's been sold out for six months!
That's great, Doc! Go ahead and enjoy yourself, and forget that you're the Number One suspect in a murder case!
KEEP OUT